The Future of Food, Money, and Work:

Charleston, SC

www.PalmettoPublishing.com

The Future of Food, Money, and Work

Copyright © 2022 by Alex Advani and Eliot Advani

Hardcover ISBN: 979-8-218-08126-3

eBook ISBN: 979-8-218-08127-0

The Future of Food, Money, and Work:

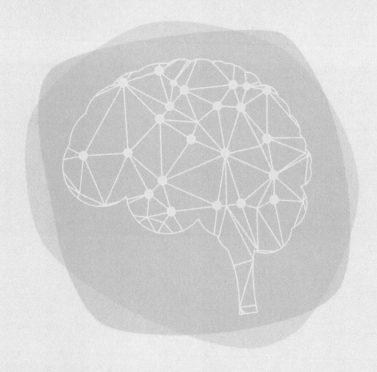

Technologies Every Kid Should Know About

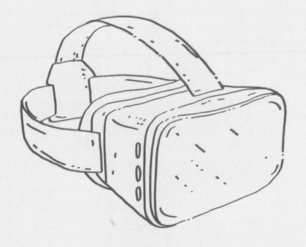

Acknowledgements

As high schoolers and twin co-authors we are something of an anomaly in terms of publishing a book. Therefore, there are several people to thank for helping us along the way.

None of this would have been possible without the inspiration and platform of our friends and peers at The Knowledge Society (TKS).

We would like to express our gratitude for Mrs. Funnell, our English teacher, and Ms. Mason, who taught Mechatronics for exposing us to new ideas.

As we turned this dream into a reality, our parents became our cheerleaders, helping us find time in our packed schedules to go the extra mile.

We would also like to thank our friends at Palmetto Publishing for their help in navigating the publishing process.

Finally, we offer a word of thanks to our illustrator, Verónica González, for putting up with our constant edits and additions without complaint.

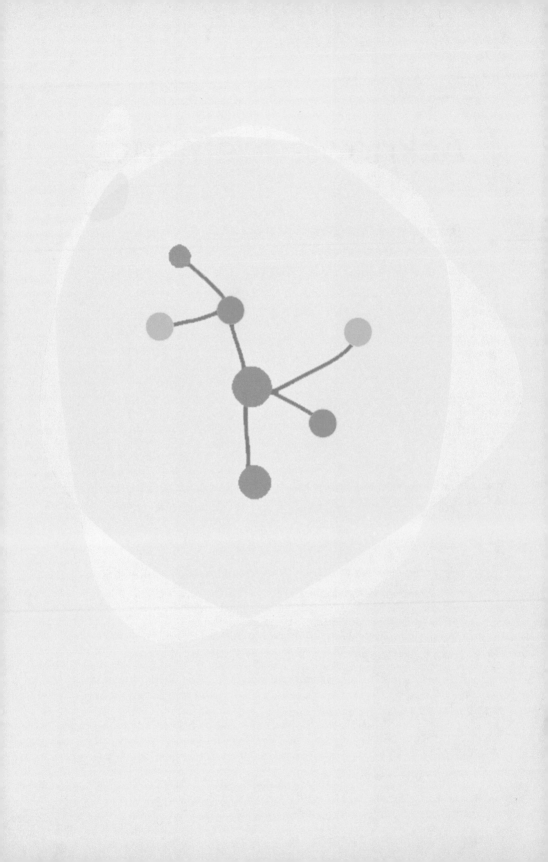

Introduction

This book is written for teenagers and pre-teens, but we hope that adults will find it interesting too. It offers a sneak peek into the future. It explains in easy-to-understand language how some of today's cutting-edge technologies will change the world as we know it. After reading this book, our wish is that you will have a head start on your peers and be inspired to learn more. Learning about these ten technologies will give you a window into the future of food, money, and work, just as it did for us.

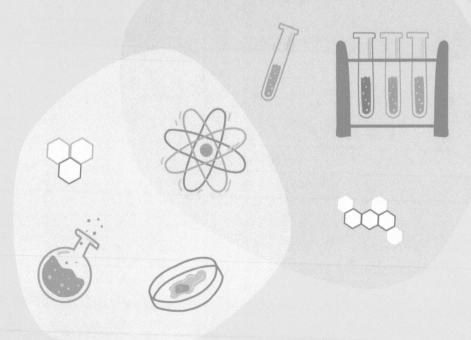

10 Technologies

1   3D PRINTING

2   CELLULAR AGRICULTURE

3   BRAIN-COMPUTER INTERFACES

4   BIONICS

5   VIRTUAL AND AUGMENTED REALITY

6   GENE EDITING

7   OPTOGENETICS

8   NANOTECH

9   INTERNET OF THINGS

10   NUCLEAR FUSION

CHAPTER 1

3D PRINTING

Charles Hull:

In 1983, Charles Hull worked for a company that used **ultraviolet lights** to make coatings for tables. The process used ultraviolet light to harden a liquid resin on top of a table, but Hull saw more potential in this process. He realized that a program on his computer could take a model of an object, slice it up into many layers, and he could recreate these layers with a similar process to the table coating. Each layer could be shaped, then hardened with UV light, creating a solid product. This process was known as stereolithography and was the first 3D printing technique. Hull's experimentation with UV lights and resin have developed rapidly and we are now able to use 3D printing technology to make anything from a boat to working body parts.

Key Terms:

Ultraviolet light - UV light is a form of light that **can't be seen by the human eye**. It is released naturally by the sun and causes sunburn.

3D Printing Organs:

Modern 3D printing is very advanced, and the newest use for this technology is creating working human body parts. This includes our organs, which are extremely important and hard to replicate. Scientists have been using 3D printers to create the shape of organs with special plastice that can safely exist in the human body. As the skeleton of the organ is created, human cells, from the patient's body, are mixed in. Once this process is complete, the cells are given time to grow, and the organ is implanted into the patient. This process is not used in hospitals yet, but **it is very promising for the future**.

How does it work?

A model of a certain object is created on a computer, and this model is sent to the 3D printer. A material, which is usually a type of plastic, is added to the printer. This material is added in layers and slowly builds up to the full desired item. The process of printing an object can be very long, especially if that object is very detailed or big.

CHAPTER 2
CELLULAR
AGRICULTURE

Discovery:

In 1912 a biologist named Alexis Carrel first proved the possibility of keeping muscle tissue alive outside of the body. Carrel's discovery was extremely unique and scientists spanning the globe were unable to copy it. As Carrel kept the culture alive for over 20 years his experiment gained more attention and credibility. Now, over a century later, thanks to his work, there are more than 50 well-established companies focused on **cellular agriculture**.

What is it?

Cellular agriculture is the production of agricultural products, such as cow meat, from cell cultures using multiple scientific methods including controlling and manipulating tissue. This technology has already begun transforming the food industry in the developed world. The concept of cellular agriculture is relatively simple; For meat products, muscle cells are harvested from the living animal and grown in the lab to create muscle tissue. Muscle tissue is the main element of the meat that we regularly consume. In order to create a full-sized burger, it takes around 20,000 strands of lab-grown muscle tissue.

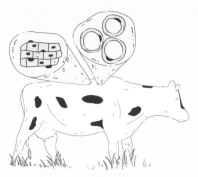

Cellular agriculture is not only more environmentally conscious and a more stable supply of food, but it also allows the exciting possibility of efficiently tailoring food to the needs of specific people. For example, someone with high cholesterol could order eggs with less cholesterol content. Milk could be lactose-free and meat could contain less fat. These innovations could make many foods more accessible and abundant.

Key Terms:

Acellular - made of organic molecules (proteins and fats) and contain no cellular or living material.
Cellular - made of living cells or once-living cells.

CHAPTER ③
BRAIN-COMPUTER INTERFACES

How it works:

Brain-Computer Interfaces (BCIs) are systems that use signals from the brain to complete an action. This means that instead of physicallypushing, moving, or pressing something, a BCI can use brain signals to complete the task, making it possible to control something with the human mind.

Every time you use one of your senses, cells in your brain called neurons shoot electrical signals to each other. Neurons are very small, and there are around 86 billion of them in the average human brain! The electrical signal passes information at incredible speeds through the brain. These signals are covered by something called Myelin, a substance that surrounds the neurons. Myelin acts as a shield to protect the rest of the brain from electric signals. However, some of these signals escape the shield of Myelin and can be picked up by a device. This is how BCIs can pick up brain signals.

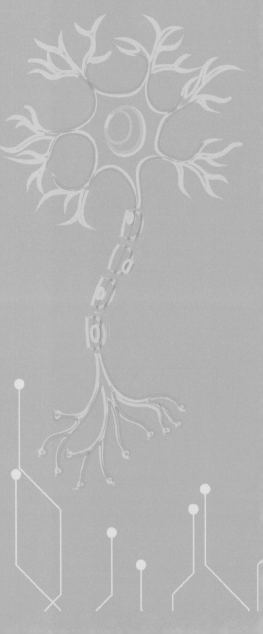

Types of BCIs:

Although BCIs seem very complicated, because the brain has so many neurons, many BCI devices are simple because of how easy it is for a device to pick up brain signals. Some even look like headbands that sit on the forehead. This type of BCI is called a non-invasive device because it is on top of the head, not inside it. Non-invasive BCIs do not require surgery to be installed and can be very easy to use.

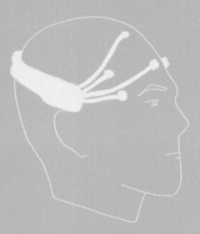

How it can help:

A new BCI technology uses the brain signals of people with ALS to help them communicate. ALS is a disease that causes people to become paralyzed and lose the ability to communicate. A man with ALS in Germany was given brain surgery, and doctors placed two devices on his brain's tissue, which could pick up his neuron's signals. This information was sent to a computer and, when he focused on an alphabet, his brain signals were converted to audio. This allowed him to communicate with his doctors, and even talk to his son.

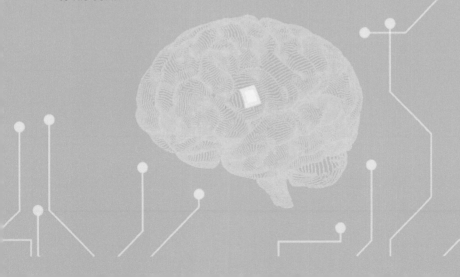

CHAPTER 4
BIONICS

Explanation:

Bionics is the science of making artificial (human-built) systems that have the same function and purpose as living systems. Bionics uses mechanics to replicate living systems and finds new, useful ideas for artificial machines. One common example of bionics is **bionic limbs**, which are artificial body parts, such as an arm or hand, that use signals from a person's muscles to move as a real limb would.

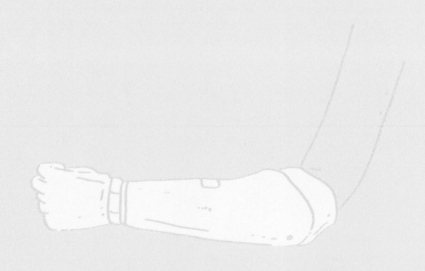

How it helps humans:

As bionics develops, there is a growing market for products that can be used to benefit the human body. This includes bionic limbs, wearable kidneys, brain prosthetics, and even bionic eyes. By copying the natural construction of human body parts, we can create body parts that work just like a natural one would. The marvels of bionics could help so many, from veterans who lost limbs, to babies born with deformities, to people who develop internal organ problems.

Innovator - Ben Ryan:

When Ben Ryan's newborn son had to have his arm amputated, he wanted to make sure that he had a prosthetic arm. He found out the hard way that prosthetics designed for younger kids were not made to be interactive or to allow hand movement. They simply used a rigid socket and a plastic hand. He decided that this wasn't good enough and decided to make his own. By using a 3-D printer, and parts of an Xbox gaming console, he was able to construct a prosthetic arm that allowed his son to move freely and grip objects. Bionics are a step up from prosthetics because they are controlled by muscle signals and even brain signals

CHAPTER 5
VIRTUAL AND AUGMENTED REALITY

Morton Heilig's Sensorama:

The sensorama, invented in 1962, by Morton Heilig, is considered to be the first virtual reality system. This machine was designed to fully immerse a viewer in a movie, by adding smells, weather simulation, and a moving seat to simulate movement. The movie was played on a wide screen as the viewer's head was covered to block out the outside world and make the viewer feel as though they were actually inside the movie.

Introducing . . .

sensorama

The Revolutionary Motion Picture System that takes you into another world with

- 3-D
- WIDE VISION
- MOTION
- COLOR
- STEREO-SOUND
- AROMAS
- WIND
- VIBRATIONS

SENSORAMA, INC., 855 GALLOWAY ST., PACIFIC PALISADES, CALIF. 90272
TEL. (213) 459-2162

How it works:

While the concept of virtual reality may seem very complicated, the idea is very simple. A virtual reality headset works like a pair of goggles. In this pair of goggles, there are two screens in front of your eyes. Within the headset, there is a sensor that alerts the technology as to what position and angle your head is in, and this allows the screens to show wherever you are looking. An example of this is if you are using the VR headset to explore the jungle. As you tilt your head to look up, the sensors will pick this movement up and seamlessly go through many frames of images, so that you can see the full forest environment around you.

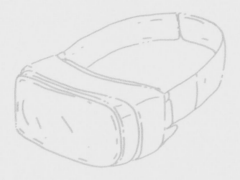

Different VR headsets:

While virtual reality is becoming more popular, it can still be difficult to get access to the newest VR technology. While many companies create high-end VR headsets with accessories, there are also many easy ways to experience the VR world for almost no money. It is possible to make your own headset for just 10 dollars, or you can purchase a cardboard headset. Compared to when VR was first introduced, we are very lucky to have such an amazing experience so easily accessible.

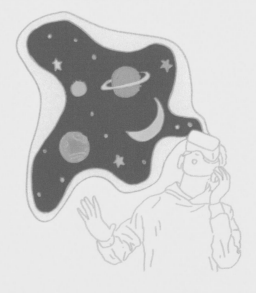

CHAPTER 6
GENE EDITING

What is it?

Simply put, genome editing is a technology designed to change an organism's DNA. We've all heard of DNA but what exactly is it, and what is its purpose? DNA is a molecule, containing all of the instructions for how our body works and looks. Every living thing, plants and animals alike, contain DNA. Genes are made up of DNA and all genes come from your parents. This is why children often look like a mix of their parents and carry the same mannerisms and, in some cases, illnesses as them. This brings us to the exciting technology that is genome editing. Imagine if we could snip away certain strands of DNA to take away any bad information that is given to our bodies, therefore eliminating certain passed-on illnesses before they can become an issue.

CRISPR:

CRISPR is the name of a genome editing technology. CRISPR targets the unwanted genome and fires an enzyme at it, causing it to break away and effectively shut off. While CRISPR is not widely used yet, it is an exciting up-and-coming technology that will lead to a whole new way to combat genetic mishaps and illnesses.

Jennifer Doudna:

Jennifer Doudna, along with Emmanuelle Charpentier, won the Nobel prize in chemistry for their discovery of CRISPR. Jennifer Doudna is the biggest name in genome editing, and for a good reason. She was the pioneer of CRISPR and worked tirelessly in the lab to make incredible discoveries such as this. Doudna grew up in Hawaii, and was always interested in nature and the outdoors, leading to her love for the sciences. She wanted to discover as much as she could about the flora and fauna she was seeing on a daily basis. Her love for biochemistry has changed the world of genome editing.

CHAPTER 7
OPTOGENETICS

Optogenetics:

Imagine being able to control your pet with a remote. You could hit a button and put your dog to sleep, or click another button and have your cat run in circles. Now imagine doing the same thing to yourself, turning off your ability to feel pain, putting yourself to sleep every night. This may become a reality with optogenetics. Optogenetics is a method of controlling what our cells do using light. While mind control sounds very cool, optogenetics is mainly used to learn what specific cells do and treat many medical conditions.

How it works:

Cells in our brains have specific jobs, and they often help us do specific actions. On the surface of these cells is something called ion channel receptors. These receptors act as an on and off switch for our cells. If we use light to control them we can control many of our body's actions by turning certain cells on and off. In order to see what certain cells influence, we can turn them off and on and run tests to see what has changed in the body.

Experiment explained:

Students from Northwestern University managed to create a bond between mice by using optogenetics. They implanted two mice with blue lights in their brains, and then put them together in a cage. Once the mice had settled in the cage, their lights were turned on, and immediately they began to bond with each other. This was because the lights were in the same place in each of their brains, and they had the same frequency. This synced up that part of each of their brains. They then tested the experiment by doing the same thing but changing the frequency of the light in one mouse. They bonded far less. By turning on the cells in each of the mice, they were able to sync up their actions and have them bond.

CHAPTER 8
NANOTECH

What is Nanotechnology?

Nanotechnology is a technology that works at the nanoscale. The nanoscale is on the scale of nanometers, which is one billionth of a meter! To put that in
perspective, human hair is 100,000 nanometers thick.
Because nanotechnology works on such a small
scale, it isn't visible and most people don't notice it.
While it still isn't possible to make functioning devices on the nanoscale, many nanomaterials are being
used and created.

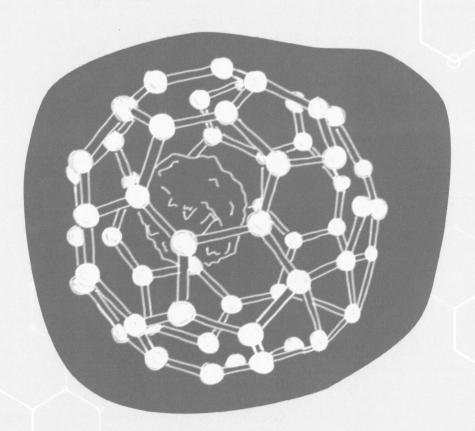

Graphene:

One of these nanomaterials is graphene, a material made up of carbon atoms. Because it is only one atom thick, graphene is on a nano-scale. Its structure is in the shape of a honeycomb, and the layer of carbon atoms is incredibly strong. In fact, graphene is two hundred times stronger than steel! Because it is so strong at a nano-scale, graphene is both flexible and very strong. Another important feature of graphene is its incredible ability to conduct electricity. To electrons, graphene is so thin that it is essentially a 2-D material. These types of materials are very rare, and graphene was the first to be discovered. 2-D materials stop electrons from moving in many directions and restrict them to a single direction.

What does this mean for the future?

Because of its hexagonal 2-D structure, graphene has very little resistance on electrons, which means that it conducts electricity very efficiently. In the future, a graphene supercapacitor could charge a phone in 5 seconds! Graphene could also be used to filter the salt out of seawater. By poking very small holes in graphene, water would go through, but other materials would not fit through the graphene sheet. This could speed up water purification processes and provide millions of people with cleaner water.

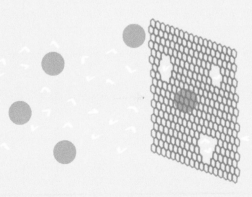

CHAPTER 9

INTERNET OF THINGS (IoT)

How It Works:

The internet of things refers to a large network of connected objects that can collect and share data. These objects could be anything from a trash can that senses when it is too heavy and needs to have its contents removed, to sneakers that track a user's steps throughout the day. These objects can give the information directly to a user, or store the data for future use, as they are on the internet. Unfortunately, this can raise security problems, because if you can control an object, such as the lock to your door, from your phone, what is to stop a hacker from getting into your house. The internet of things will grow extremely fast, and with it will come unimaginable possibilities.

IoT and self-driving cars:

Imagine you are driving around a city and your car can navigate you around pedestrians, other cars, and traffic lights, even finding you an open parking spot nearby. All of this is achievable thanks to IoT, as the connectivity of all devices and objects around us can open a world of possibilities. If cars are able to connect and communicate with each other it is even possible that one day we could completely eliminate traffic lights.

CHAPTER 10
NUCLEAR FUSION

How it works:

As you know, pollution and global warming are changing the world. They not only affect the weather, but also our food supply, rising sea levels, and much more. The biggest cause of global warming is greenhouse gases, produced by the burning of fossil fuels to create energy. By collecting these fossil fuels, we are ruining the environment, but until now there has been no solution to the need for effective sustainable, clean energy. Nuclear fusion has the possibility of creating a never-ending source of energy in the near future.

Current energy sources cause too much pollution

How it works:

The process of nuclear fusion is the collision between two atomic particles. These minuscule particles join together upon collision to create a bigger particle and produce a massive amount of energy in this process. The way that this is used to create energy lies in the amount of heat that is produced by the collision. This extreme heat is up to seven times hotter than the sun or over 100 million degrees!

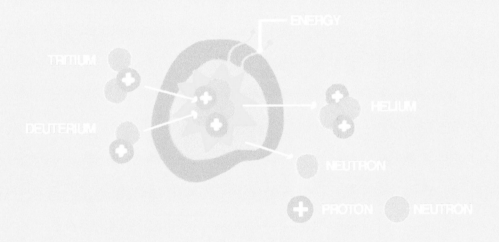

Conclusion

Each of the technologies mentioned in this book will influence our future and be a part of your daily life as you grow up. Companies and nonprofit organizations are shaping the future of food, money, and work by creating new exciting projects all around the world to further the development of these technologies. It is our wish that this book has sparked your curiosity to learn more and make a real difference by applying one or more of the technologies that we have described. We hope that you have found inspiration in these chapters, just as writing this book did for us, to deepen your knowledge and even start projects of your own to build our shared future.

CPSIA information can be obtained
at www.ICGtesting.com
Printed in the USA
BVHW012211140223
658549BV00009B/172/J